FRESH FLOWER ARRANGING

■ A Step by Step Guide ■

Wendy Gardiner

■ Flower Arrangements by JUNE LOVELL ■

Contents

Introduction

Flower arranging is a combination of expertise, artistry (eye for design) and experience. Flower arrangements have the wonderful advantage of looking extravagant, yet they are easy and economical to create. One or two sprays of flowers, carefully separated and positioned harmoniously with complementary foliage, can result in admirable displays. Inspiration can be gleaned from many sources and no two arrangements can, or should, be identical. Our 35 projects offer a choice of arrangements to suit every occasion, from the birth of a baby to grand celebration dinners, from gift posies to festive occasions.

Fresh Flower Arranging is intended to be a practical guide, taking each project step by step to its completion. It aims to use containers that are easily adapted, as well as everyday objects that are readily available in most homes. Once you have tried these easy-to-follow projects and learned the basic skills, you will be ready to enjoy experimenting: altering these arrangements simply by substituting your own choice of flowers or colour combinations, and also developing your own ideas.

As a flower unfolds, let this book unfold, to reveal the many delights of flower arranging and the tips that make it easy!

The Basics

EQUIPMENT

Some basic equipment will help to make your designs easier to create and look professional. All the materials below are available from good florists and it is worth investing in them before you begin.

Floral Foam

Green floral foam is used for fresh flower arrangements, while the pale brown foam is for dry and fabric flower arrangements. The green

Flower arranging materials.

variety is purchased in brick-like blocks which can be easily cut to size. The foam must always be thoroughly soaked with clean water prior to use; without this soaking, the foam will not be solid enough to hold the stems firmly. The brown foam, however, is more dense and solid and should always be used dry.

Floral Fix

This is also dark green and is a malleable Plasticine-type substance available on rolls. It is used to stick bowls firmly into baskets, or frogs into bowls and so on, firmly anchoring the arrangement in the chosen container. Indeed, it will stick most dry surfaces together, although it is not particularly effective on glass or highly-glazed surfaces.

Frogs

Sometimes known as an oasis pin, spike or prong, the frog is a small plastic disc with four spikes. It is extremely useful for holding the floral foam in place, using the fix to anchor it to the container. First place a piece of fix on the bottom of the frog, press this to the container and then impale the soaked floral foam on the frog to ensure the arrangement will be firmly held in place.

Stub Wires

Stub wires are available in a range of lengths and gauges (thicknesses). They are used to repair broken stems, hold ribbon bows or wire clusters of stems together. In intricate bouquets, they are used to hold flowers in a permanent shape.

Adhesive or Florist Tape

Florist tape is used to wrap stub wires or foam blocks to containers. It is green, to blend with the foliage, and should be wrapped around stub wires used for ribbon trims to prevent water seeping up the wire and damaging the ribbon.

Pinholders

A pinholder is a round, flat, heavy weight, with pins protruding from the base. Available in a variety of sizes, a pinholder is used to hold top-heavy floral arrangements with thick woody stems or branches. A round holder, about 2½in (6.5cm) in diameter, is the most useful size to start with.

Secateurs

Secateurs are used to cut heavy stems, branches and foliage from the garden. Avoid using on stub wire as this will blunt them very quickly.

Scissors and Knife

Scissors, preferably florist's scissors which have a serrated edge, are used to cut stems and foliage prior to placing in the arrangement. A sharp knife is also useful to cut the floral foam block to size, trimming the edges to fit. Also use the knife to slit stems of flowers, thus allowing more surface area for the water to draw up the stem.

ADDITIONAL MATERIALS

Cut Flower Food

Sold in small packets of powder or as a dilutable liquid essence, cut flower food is used to prolong the life of flowers. The solution also contains a germ inhibitor which helps keep the water pure.

Spray and Watering Can

It is advisable to top up flower arrangements with a little water every day. When inserting the floral foam into a container, leave a small space at the rear for additional daily watering.

A spray is handy, particularly in warm weather or centrally heated houses, as a daily misting will help to keep blooms really fresh and attractive.

Colour Sprays

Used sparingly to enhance a display, a colour spray can alter the look of a container, candle and so on. Special coloured sprays for flowers are also available from florists and can be used to enhance or alter the original colour of the flowers.

Ribbons

Florist ribbon, generally made from Polypropylene, is easy to work with as it folds, creases, holds its shape, does not fray and is water resistant. Woven ribbon can be used as effectively, but must be protected from water by wrapping stub wire stems with water repellent adhesive tape.

O-Bowl

A square O-bowl can be used to sit inside larger holders that it would be impractical to try and fill completely with flowers. It is also ideal for containers, such as baskets, that are not watertight.

Base

Using a base can protect furniture from possible water damage and add another dimension to the arrangement. A base, covered with co-ordinating fabric, should enhance the design. Choose a shape that complements the arrangement. Cake boards make good bases, covered according to your choice. Stands, such as teapot stands, trivets, wrought-iron display stands or cake stands, add height to an arrangement and are particularly good for displays that include flowing, trailing foliage.

Containers

All around the house are pots, crockery, glassware and containers that can be utilized imaginatively as bases for floral displays. Shallow containers, which can be virtually anything, are

Use household pots, crockery and glassware as containers.

easily hidden by the arrangement. Unleash your creativity and put the ashtray to good use! When using large containers, such as troughs, stand a smaller saucer on a brick to make it easier to arrange the flowers and prevent the arrangement from being too large and ungainly.

ACCESSORIES

Adding figurines, candles or other ornaments can add another dimension to a flower arrangement. Choose carefully, however, to ensure the ornament does not dominate the display.

Florist Bow

The bow size will depend on the length of ribbon used. As a basic guideline, however, cut a length of ribbon about 18in (45cm) long. Starting 6in (15cm) from one end, make a loop about 1in (4cm), pinch and twist to the main piece at the centre, and twist the long end between finger and thumb to keep the ribbon facing the correct way. Make a further three loops in the same manner, pinching and twisting at the centre each time. Next, twist the centre with bound stub wire to hold in place. Once fixed, arrange the loops to the shape desired and then cut off excess ribbon.

Multi-Ribbon Bow

The decorative ribbon bows often used on bouquets are actually quite simple to make. Take 10ft (3m) of florist ribbon, roll it into a flat 6in (15cm) band, leaving one end about 16in (40cm) long. Tear another yard (metre) length into ½in (1cm) wide strips. Hold the centre of the band together and cut from the outer edges diagonally towards the centre, on either side, leaving ½in (1cm) in the centre to hold together. Take a tie piece and tie around the centre very tightly, leaving two ends to secure the flower to the bouquet. Then, holding one side between the thumb and forefinger of one hand, pull the centre loop out, pull firmly and twist down with the other hand. Repeat with the next inner loop, pulling and twisting upward. Continue with each loop, pulling and twisting one down and the next one up, until all loops are pulled out. Repeat the opposite side in the same way.

CHOOSING AND PREPARING FLOWERS

Buying Flowers

Go to florists, garden centres or nurseries that are known to you or that have been recommended. Look around before you buy to see how well the various flowers are stored. A smell of decayed plant probably indicates careless handling.

All plant material should look and smell fresh. Choose blooms that are still young, in bud or about to open. The more expensive flowers should have been conditioned and fed by the florist. While cheaper bunches are not necessarily being fed, they should still be well watered, sprayed regularly if left outside in the hot sun and protected from unhealthy extremes of temperature.

Street vendors are an alternative for cheaper bunches. Go to one who has a regular pitch as they will, of course, be as anxious to please as a shop. Ideal for hardier flowers, such as carnations, chrysanthemums and so on, a good street vendor will turn the stock around quickly, keeping a regular fresh supply. Again, make sure the stock is crisp, fresh and preferably with some buds.

Garden Flowers

Using flowers grown yourself is obviously the most economical way as you only pick exactly what you need. If you do not have a range of suitable flowers, do still look for ivy, holly, ferns, leatherleaf or even yucca leaves. Pick them either in the early morning or evening when transpiration is at its lowest, and soak them immediately in a bucket of water.

Conditioning

Conditioning is the care and attention that flowers need before being used in an arrangement. Whether purchased or picked yourself, it is advisable to condition them to extend their life and improve their appearance.

Fill a bucket with about 8in (20cm) of lukewarm water and add flower food or alternatively a teaspoon of sugar. Using a sharp knife or scissors, re-cut stems at a 45-degree angle to give a greater surface area for drinking. As you cut, strip any lower leaves from the stems. Where applicable lower thorns should also be removed to prevent them damaging other

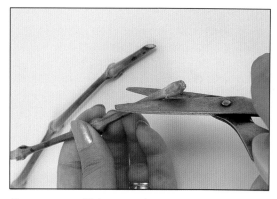

Cut stems at a 45-degree angle.

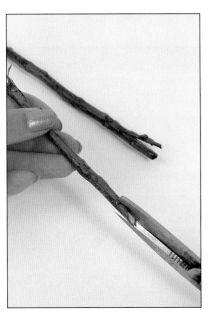

Split woody stems about ½in (1cm).

Crush stem ends of thick woody foliage to aid water absorption.

Pull off lower leaves to prevent rotting.

Gently fold outer petals back to open the bloom.

Pinch out the stamen if the colour contrast is not required or to prevent damage to furniture.

Stick a small piece of floral fix to the base of the frog to anchor it in the container.

flowers and also to make the stems easier to handle. To remove thorns use a knife blade held almost flat against the stem and chop each thorn away.

Foliage also benefits from conditioning. Green foliage should be thoroughly soaked by submerging in cold water for several hours. Yellow foliage and leaves with hairy or velvety textures should not be submerged, however, but left to stand in shallow water. Avoid letting yellow leaves come into contact with cold water as they will turn brown. Grey foliage must be kept as dry as possible; if saturated it will lose its colour as well as siphon water from the container and drip on its surroundings, potentially ruining both arrangement and furniture. To condition grey leaves re-cut the stems, stripping the lower leaves. Wrap the remaining leaves in a cloth to protect them and plunge the stems into boiling water for about 20 seconds and then stand the ends in shallow cold water until ready to use.

General Tips

- Cut stems, preferably under water, immediately prior to using. Cut at a 45-degree angle and slit about ¾in (2cm) to increase the drinking surface. Woody stems, such as roses, should then be beaten with a hammer to crush the end.
- Many leaves and sprays of leaves can be submerged prior to use and then stood upright in water until required. However, never submerge grey foliage (see above).
- Leave flowers and foliage soaking upright in a bucket of water for several hours. Keep in water until ready to use.
- Remove thorns and leaves from the lower parts of stems or they will drink more than their share of water. They will be discarded later anyway.
- Wild flowers lose moisture rapidly so it is advisable to wrap stems in a damp cloth or newspaper immediately they are cut. Avoid handling too much as body heat will cause them to deteriorate. As soon as possible, re-cut the stems and soak in water before using.

Flowers to Look For

All Year: Chrysanthemums; Spray Chrysanthemums; Carnations; Spray Carnations; Roses.

Spring Flowers: (available all year but better when in season): Iris; *Alstroemeria*; Anemone; Freesia; Lily; Tulips and Daffodils (in season only).

Summer: Orchids; Pinks; Scabiosa; Gerbera; Monto Casino; Solidaster; *Gladiolus*; *Gypsophila*; *Delphinium*; Cream *Lilium* 'Mont Blanc'.

Foliage: Leatherleaf fern; Ruscus; Eucalyptus; *Brodiaea*.

GOOD DESIGN

Although successful flower arranging is a result of both skill and experience, there are one or two guidelines that can help you achieve visually stunning arrangements even if you are still a beginner.

Balance

An arrangement is balanced when the visual weight (eye-catching detail), on either side of an imaginary central vertical line is equal. The design should not tilt in any direction, it should flow. Generally, it is best to use dark colours lower down, place thinner pieces at the top and outer edges and position the heaviest flowers in the centre.

Proportion

The proportion is the relative size and shape of each bloom to each other and the container. The height of the arrangement should be approximately 1½–2 times the largest dimension of the container. For a horizontal design, the proportion should be 2–4 times the width or length. For a design prepared specifically for a stand, aim for two-thirds of the arrangement to be above the container and one-third draping below.

Line baskets with a polythene bag to prevent water seeping through.

Wedge the soaked foam on to the anchored frog.

Slice any excess foam away using a knife.

Rhythm or Harmony

Choose containers to match the arrangement: a curved container for a curving fluid arrangement, an angular pot for a straighter display. Use complementary colours, textures that blend or natural contrasts such as rough–smooth, light–dark.

Focal Point

Make the focal point just below the highest placement. Use the most vivid colours, the largest or most striking blooms. Surround this with the largest leaves to draw the eye to the focal point. All lines should converge on this point, which should also be the most densely filled area.

Shape and Texture

There are four basic shapes to choose from: horizontal symmetrical or asymmetrical, and vertical symmetrical or asymmetrical. Always bear in mind the balance and proportion, and decide before beginning the arrangement which basic line you wish to follow, and keep in mind the ultimate width and height.

Use the textural surface of different plants and flowers to emphasize their detail as well as the detail of neighbouring flowers.

Wedge blocks of foam in the container to fill the base, leaving only a watering gap.

PROJECT 1

Red Shoe News

- Spray Carnations
- Spray Roses
- Singapore Orchids
- Ivy
- Fern
- Pepperomia Leaves

TIPS

- Always remove lower leaves so that only the stems go into the floral foam. This prevents the leaves rotting in the foam and smelling unpleasant. It will also help to ensure there is enough room in the foam for the flower stems.
- Leave a small space at the back of the container for daily watering.
- Always cut stems at an angle, providing them with a larger surface for drinking water. Woody stems should be crushed with a hammer.

Prepare your equipment: frog, fix, soaked floral foam, stub wires, ribbons, and container, such as this little red shoe. Choose the flowers and foliage to complement the container; in this case small flowers in reds, pinks and creams. Stick floral fix to the frog and press firmly to the shoe. Impale the soaked foam, leaving about ¾in (2cm) standing proud and a gap at the back for daily watering.

Using the foliage, start the outline of the arrangement. To achieve the correct balance, the arrangement should be 1½ times the height of the container. Follow the shoe shape, placing the tallest stems at the heel. Cover as much of the floral foam surface as possible, so that the foam becomes invisible whilst allowing the shoe to be seen.

USES
The choice of red flowers and red shoe make this an ideal arrangement for ruby weddings or St Valentine's Day. Alternatively, use to celebrate passing a driving test or dancing exam.

Follow the line created by the foliage with the outer layer of spray carnations. Use the buds and smallest flowers at the outer edges and higher point and the larger blooms at the centre. Carefully place each flower so that it will always remain visible. Cut the stems at an angle, giving them as large a surface area for drinking as possible.

Split the large stem of the Singapore orchid to obtain single flowers. To do this, cut just above each orchid stem so that each flower retains part of the main stem to anchor into the foam. Use the remaining top length of the stem, with orchid buds, to emphasise the line of the display and create the highest point of the arrangement.

Add the cream/white spray roses down the centre of the arrangement. Before placing, open out the petals of larger blooms by gently blowing into them. Cut the stem to the lengths required and split the ends. Strip away the lower leaves and use as foliage if required. Use the smaller roses at the top, gradually working down, placing the largest flower at the central focal point.

Add the ribbon bows for the final touch and celebrate!

Summer Garden

- Spray Carnations
- Carnations
- Roses
- Fuchsia
- Single Spray Chrysanthemums
- Lavender
- Sedum Spectabile
- Larkspur

Anchor a block of soaked floral foam to a frog fixed into the base of the bowl. Then, slice off a third and wedge it down one side. Add another small block of foam to the other side. Place a tall stem of larkspur at the centre back, one either side and one centre front placed horizontally. Add more larkspur to define the rounded shape, working down both sides and the front.

Once the outline has been created, add four or five sprigs of fuchsia around the base, placing each sprig horizontally so that it will drape gracefully. Then add stems of lavender either side of the centre back larkspur, working down either side and around the front, following the line of the arrangement.

Cut the carnation stems to slightly different lengths, place one either side of the centre back and then work down the sides and front, following the shape and allowing the lower carnations to drape downwards. Continue to fill out the centre and front with sprigs of *Sedum spectabile*, pushing the stems deep into the foam, and again varying the lengths.

Split the stems and strip away the lower leaves of three roses before adding them to the front of the arrangement. Next add complete stems of spray carnations, cut to different lengths. Work round the arrangement, adding the spray carnations as appropriate to fill any gaps, placing the lower blooms at a horizontal angle to follow the outline.

Continue to fill out the roundness of the arrangement using single chrysanthemums. Place the tallest spray towards the centre back, with the shorter stems at the front. Add three large roses to the centre front, again starting with the tallest at the back. Finally, add stems of spray roses to the centre, filling any small gaps still remaining.

Pinks in Boots

- Roses
- Nerines
- Gerbera Daisies
- Alstroemeria
- Single Chrysanthemums
- Pinks
- Ivy
- Pink Berry Pernetia

TIPS

- To strengthen the stems of weaker foliage, wind stub wire around the stem to the desired height.
- To aid water absorption split woody stems, especially roses, and lightly crush the end. Soft stems should be cut at an angle of 45 degrees.
- Open petals of roses by gently blowing into the heads.

This black boot container, although small, has a 'heavy' look so larger flowers will suit it best. You will also need a soaked floral foam block, florist tape, fix, frog, stub wires, paper ribbon and scissors.

Stick the frog inside the boot and then wedge the block of saturated floral foam firmly on to the frog, leaving about 1¼in (3cm) standing proud. Also leave a small gap behind the foam for daily watering. Clip the ivy into manageable lengths, taking off the lower leaves to 'clean' them, and place the ivy and the pernetia in the foam following the line of the boot.

Choose each flower carefully, bearing in mind the natural curve of the stem when placing it in the arrangement. Add flowers in groups, placing the longer stems at the back. Cutting the stems at an angle not only provides a larger surface area for drinking, it also makes them easier to poke into the foam. Follow the shape of the container to create the line of the arrangement.

The next group of flowers, the carnations and pinks, are added to the left side. Starting with carnations, trim the stems and strip the lower leaves away before placing them. Cut each bloom to different heights, filling out the display as you work. Add the pinks to the carnation groups as they belong to the same family. Leave the buds on to bloom later.

Use single chrysanthemums to fill in any gaps. Crush the stem ends to help water soak up to the heads. Add the *Alstroemeria* by cutting the flowers from the main stem at an angle, leaving the top leaf and buds on. Place them in groups of colours, using different heights to create depth. Add paper ribbon bows held with bound stub wire to prevent water damage.

Add loops of paper ribbon, twisted together with taped stub wire.

PROJECT 4

American Posy

- Solidaster
- Double Tulip
- Spray Chrysanthemums
- Carnations
- Leatherleaf Fern
- Croton leaves

Place a small piece of floral fix on the bottom of the frog and press firmly into the vase. Cut the soaked foam to size and, leaving a watering gap, press on to the frog to anchor in place. Starting with foliage, with stems cut at an angle, position the leatherleaf fern round the base to form the rounded outline of this American-style posy.

Cover the remainder of the foam surface, using all the leaves. Use the smaller fronds to cover the centre; first stripping the bottom leaves from each stem to prevent them rotting in the foam, then laying them across the foam and inserting the stems diagonally. Add the *Solidaster*, maintaining the shape with the shorter bushier lengths in the centre.

Prepare double tulips by opening some of the flowers. To do this, run your thumb lightly down the back of each petal, gently turning it outwards. Also use some tulips in bud for contrast. Cut to length, strip lower leaves and insert in the rounded shape. Alternate opened tulip and bud, keeping the arrangement symmetrical. Add a central carnation to define the final height.

Fill in any remaining gaps with spray chrysanthemums. Use every flower separately, pushing between the tulips, gradually filling out to create the desired shape. Add more foliage, if necessary, to balance the arrangement.

Add croton leaves for colour contrast and to fill any gaps. Working symmetrically, add the main carnations around the central carnation of the posy, varying the heights in order to keep to the rounded shape. Blow gently into carnation heads to open slightly if necessary.

PROJECT 5

Celebration Dinner

Wedge a floral foam block firmly into the centre of a square O-bowl. Add the foliage round the outer edge to begin the elongated shape planned. Place a sprig of *Euphorbia* into either side to define the width. Always strip lower leaves from stems before pushing into the foam as this will prevent decay.

Cut candles to vary the height and push carefully into the foam. Keep candle wicks well above the tallest flower to avoid fire. Cover the remaining foam surface with leather-leaf fronds, placed diagonally, and add more *Euphorbia* to the front and rear to balance the shape. Add a small upright sprig to contrast with the white candles.

Add more short lengths of *Euphorbia* around the candles, continuing to cover the floral foam. Cut small sprigs of *Gypsophila* from the main stem and insert round the base, filling out the shape. Add as many sprigs as necessary to give a good balance.

Add the main flowers – the single spray daisies – positioning them so that they bend naturally. Use all the buds round the bottom to drape attractively over the stand. Place the open flowers in a diagonal line from either side, working up to the candles to provide a focal point. Add a similar line from front to rear, working round the display so that all angles are equally pleasing.

- Euphorbia
- Gypsophila
- White single Daisy Chrysanthemums
- Ivy leaves
- Eucalyptus
- Leatherleaf fern

TIPS
- If candles have a tendency to lean, shore them up with short stems of leatherleaf which will remain hidden.
- Spray *Gypsophila* with coloured floral spray in order to blend it with your chosen colour scheme.

Make ribbon bows, looping six or seven times if you are using softer narrow ribbon in order to add fullness to the bow. Pinch and twist each loop between thumb and forefinger, binding loops with taped stub wire. Add to the display as desired.

Place the arrangement on a stand so that *Euphorbia* and daisies drape attractively or, alternatively, let them run along a table.

PROJECT 6

Country Basket

- Trelicium
- Phlox Rose
- Spray Roses
- Micro Carnations
- Pink Freesia
- Blue Scabiosa
- Lavender Monto Casino
- Silver Leaf

Line the basket with waterproof material, such as a polythene bag, attaching it to the basket with floral fix. Add another piece of fix to the inside of the bag and press frog firmly in place. Cut the soaked floral foam to size and impale on frog. Choose the flowers to complement the proposed arrangement; here a natural bunched display is planned.

Start with the silver leaf and lavender monto casino, inserted horizontally on one side to represent a bunch of flowers. Next add the micro carnations, again virtually horizontally. Intersperse with *Trelicium* and blue *Scabiosa*, bringing the line up gently, and use shorter stems of freesia and phlox roses placed more vertically to round the floral side of the arrangement.

Add more layers of all the flowers, bringing them round and up into a wider, full posy shape. Cut spray roses down, using the top buds, flowers and leaves. Add upright sprays to the other side of the basket handle, continuing to cover the floral foam surface.

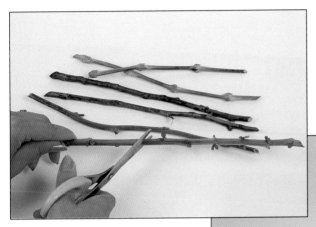

Strip any remaining leaves off the stalks left from the flowers and foliage already used. Cut each stem to about 8in (20cm), varying the lengths slightly to create a more natural look. Then cut the stems at each end to a 45-degree angle.

Place the stems in the right side of the basket to create the illusion of a bunch of flowers laid across the basket. Insert the first few horizontally, matching the flowers opposite. Round the arrangement by layering stalks, bringing some up towards the centre.

Add the paper bow to the centre as if wrapped around the stems.

Golden Pedestal

Cut two bricks of soaked floral foam into three blocks, varying the size of each to create different heights. Using a frog fixed to the base of the container, anchor the largest block in the centre. Wedge the two smaller pieces either side, packing them in tightly, and leaving just a small watering gap.

Trim the lower leaves from stems of dyed oak leaves before inserting into the soaked foam. Start the basic triangular shape with a tall stem at the back, equal lengths either side and slightly shorter ones at the front. Add stag's horn sumach and yellow berried *Pyracantha* symmetrically.

- Peach Gladiolus
- Orange Lily
- Yellow Gerbera
- Orange Carnations
- Red single Chrysanthemums
- Spray Fantasy Carnations
- Mimosa
- Dyed Oak Leaves
- Yellow Berried Pyracantha
- Hypericum (St John's wort)
- Stag's Horn Sumach

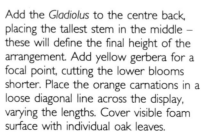

TIPS
- If you want *Gladiolus* to stand straight, pinch out the top tips.
- It is easier to work in lines when placing each flower group.
- Push stems well into the floral foam, about 1¼ in (3cm), to anchor them firmly.

Add the *Gladiolus* to the centre back, placing the tallest stem in the middle — these will define the final height of the arrangement. Add yellow gerbera for a focal point, cutting the lower blooms shorter. Place the orange carnations in a loose diagonal line across the display, varying the lengths. Cover visible foam surface with individual oak leaves.

Remove pollen stamens from the lilies (to prevent them from staining furniture), before placing them in a central line through the arrangement. Add the mimosa to the right-hand side, between dyed oak leaves to emphasize the colour of each. Balance on the left with St John's wort, again placing between dyed oak leaves for the best effect.

To finish the display add spray chrysanthemums, filling in any gaps still remaining. For a touch of luxury, add large golden bows and one or two strips of gold florist paper looped and opened slightly. Secure with taped stub wires to prevent water damage to the ribbon. The golden ribbon also adds warmth to the beautiful autumnal colours.

Stand the display on a brass pedestal to complement the colours and pick out the golden ribbons.

Cosy Candlelight

- White Monto Casino
- Champagne Spray Roses
- Peach Roses
- Spray Carnations
- Leatherleaf fern
- Silver leaf

Place a circular piece of soaked floral foam in each candle cup. Then, cut a fern into individual fronds and position round the lower edge of the foam. In between, add the points of white monto casino and fill in with the remainder of the flowers from the stem. Work up the sides of the foam, adding one small sprig of monto casino to the top. Add small end stems of silver leaf to fill gaps around the base.

Using small peach roses, work in a diagonal line from the top of the display down the side. Pick off outer petals to balance both sides if necessary. Use a small bud in the centre, then larger blooms. Now add champagne spray roses as the next layer of the base. Cut each small bud and rose and insert separately, bringing the larger roses to the centre of each display.

Use candle cups for this candelabra display. Place a piece of floral fix on the outside base of the cups and push into the candle holders. Add another piece of fix to the inside centre of each cup and press a frog firmly into each one. Put an appropriately coloured candle in the centre stem of the candelabra. As this arrangement is for an intimate supper, use smaller flowers, cut quite short for a simple line.

Insert individual carnations, cut from the spray carnations, between the peach and champagne roses, cutting stems to different lengths in order to fill out the roundness of each display. Push firmly into the floral foam to anchor in position. Finally, finish with two small co-ordinating bows in each cup.

PROJECT 9

Go Dutch

TIP
● Make bear grass into decorative loops using three strands of grass looped together and secured with silver wire. Add to the arrangement with the long ends at the top.

● Cream Lilies
● Cream Carnations
● Cream Spray Carnations
● Yellow Tulips
● Ivy leaves
● Lichen Moss
● Bear Grass
● Hexenine (Mind-your-own-business)

Cut a soaked foam brick to the size of the dish, leaving a small watering gap, and fix it in place with a frog. Remove the lower leaves from the three main lilies, cut each to a different height and place in the left side of the foam in a group. Trim ivy leaves and position individually around the base of the lilies to cover the foam.

Cover the foam centre with lichen moss anchored in place with pins made from 2in (5cm) lengths of stub wire bent into hairpin shape. Add three carnations, cut to different heights, next to the lilies. Place them carefully, so that they naturally face forward.

Add spray carnations at a slightly lower height than the other carnations, placing the tallest at the back. Cover the foam below with mind-your-own-business, pinned in place with the stub wire pins. Add more spray carnations, keeping within the group and cutting those for the front shorter to keep the shape.

Variation: Take out the group of carnations and replace with blue iris, again grouping them together. As before, cut the stems to different lengths to maintain the shape. Add four mini *Cymbiodium* orchids to the lower left and two or three *Brodiaea* below the iris.

Add more ivy leaves to the right end to cover the foam. Trim tulips to size, strip lower leaves and insert on the right side at an angle in the foam so that they fall naturally. Finally add three bear grass loops together with two or three stems of straight bear grass to give a softer edge to the line.

Barrowful of Blooms

- Blue Delphiniums
- Blue Iris
- Mauve Monto Casino
- Brodiaea
- Anemones
- Blue Statice
- Eucalyptus leaves
- Ivy leaves
- Tradescantia

Place one or two pieces of bark in front of the display to accentuate the rustic feel.

TIPS
- Use cuttings from houseplants such as *Tradescantia* as foliage. They will add colour and texture.
- Use a margarine or ice-cream carton to line the basket.

Line the wheelbarrow with a waterproof liner, such as a polythene bag cut to size. Snugly fit a soaked floral foam into the lining, secured by a frog. Add stems of monto casino at right angles round the base and intersperse with eucalyptus leaves, letting them fall naturally. Working from the centre, add a diagonal line of ivy leaves for textural interest.

Cut blue delphinium stems at an angle and insert into the left of the foam at a slightly higher angle than the monto casino, gradually building up the shape. To the right add blue iris, trimmed to

varying heights. Strip the lower leaves and insert at an angle, gently working up towards the centre with shorter stems.

Add *Tradescantia* to the lower left corner for colour. Insert another delphinium at a straighter angle to balance the shape. Then use *Brodiaea* to fill in and create the final outline, before adding the centre flowers. Use more eucalyptus leaves to cover any visible foam.

Add the anemones to create the focal point. Trim each stem at an angle and to different lengths. Rest small bits of bark amongst the arrangement or upon foliage. Add one or two stems of blue statice to fill out the centre. Finally, insert a long stem of eucalyptus leaves to the back, together with two sprays of blue statice to soften the line.

PROJECT 11

Oriental Mews

Use a wide, shallow dish to create this oriental-style arrangement. Make sure the dish is dry before using. Put two frogs, secured with floral fix, into either side of the dish. Clean and dry some pebbles, gather together dry fungi and bamboo canes. Soak two blocks of floral foam and impale firmly on each frog.

- Anthurium
- Pale Pink Nerine
- Castor Oil Plant Leaves
- Bear Grass
- Anthurium Leaves
- Lichen Moss
- Natural Fungi

Make the bamboo frame using fresh bamboo sticks or any substitute preferred. Tie two pieces at right angles using silver florist wire covered with florist tape. Add more bamboo to form a grid, securing each cross-section. Cut the horizontal ends to 45-degree angles to show the hollow bamboo. Tie any remaining bamboo ends, cut to different lengths, into a bundle.

Anchor the bamboo frame into both floral foams and then push the bundle of bound sticks into the left side. Cover both foam bases with fungi and lichen moss using stub wire bent into 'pins'. Next, add an anthurium leaf to the left foam and two castor oil plant leaves to the right foam. Loop a strand of bear grass, add to the back of the right foam and then fill the dish with cleaned pebbles.

Pierce a piece of fungi with stub wire and add to the back of the left foam. Place one anthurium, cut very short, next to the anthurium leaf already positioned. Add a long-stemmed anthurium next to the tallest bamboo pole and then two others at different heights to complete the line. Add a final anthurium to the left, letting it fall naturally.

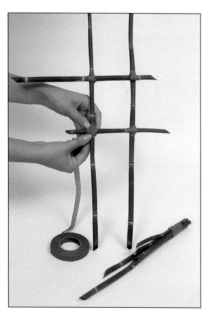

TIPS
- Add a sachet of crystals to purify the water.
- Spray the leaves with leaf shine for added depth of colour.

Cut three nerines to different, short lengths and add to the right foam in a loose line. Bind five stems of bear grass with silver wire and insert next to the looped one, then add two single stems cut to size. Finally, loop two stems and add at right angles to finish the line.

Pour in enough water to cover the stones, and float a nerine head in the dish.

PROJECT 12

Duck Designs

- Anemones
- Cream Carnations
- Grape Hyacinths (Muscari)
- Singapore Orchids
- Spray Carnations
- Ivy Leaves
- Boston Fern

Line the basket with a waterproof lining, such as a polythene bag, and into it wedge a soaked floral foam cut to size, leaving about 1¼ in (3cm) standing proud. At the tail end of the duck-shaped container use ivy leaves and Boston fern to simulate the tail. Add more ivy leaves following the shape of the basket.

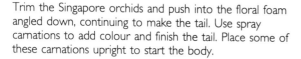

Trim the Singapore orchids and push into the floral foam angled down, continuing to make the tail. Use spray carnations to add colour and finish the tail. Place some of these carnations upright to start the body.

Working from the front, add four carnations to the centre angling them slightly to the rear. Next group some *Muscari* horizontally round the neck end, keeping the head and wings visible and using ivy leaves as a backdrop. Use groups of the discarded *Muscari* leaves, bound together with stub wire, to fill out the body of the arrangement.

If required use more spray carnations to fill any gaps. Then add anemones to the body, placing in a group next to the main focal point (the carnations). Leave the top leaves in place, removing only the lower leaves to prevent them rotting in the foam.

Country Garden

- Blue Delphiniums
- Astilbe
- Lavender Monto Casino
- Blue Iris
- Pink Stocks
- Pink Carnations
- Deep Pink Roses
- Spray Carnations
- Dyed Dill
- Eucalyptus
- Ruscus
- Silver Leaf

When using a large vase, either use an extra floral foam to build it up, leaving at least 5in (13cm) standing proud, or use a smaller vase gently lowered inside. Starting with the foliage, outline the tri-angular shape of the arrangement with *Ruscus* at the bottom left, eucalyptus at the top right and silver leaf at the bottom right.

Choose a strong stem of blue delphinium, cut the end at a 45-degree angle and place in front of the tallest *Ruscus*. Use two other delphiniums, cut to slightly different lengths, either side of the first one. Place the *Astilbe* in a varied group at the lower left and balance at the opposite top right with a second grouping.

Add the blue iris buds and flowers to the left of the arrangement, inserting each stem, devoid of lower leaves, at different angles. Add one stem to the right of centre, working a slightly diagonal line through the centre. Next add a row of pink carnations.

Working from side to side, fill in the shape using pink stocks. Then add a single stem of dark pink roses, in a loose diagonal line opposite the carnations. Insert two or three stems of lavender monto casino to balance the *Astilbe* and finally a few sprigs of spray-dyed dill to complete the focal point. Add a ribbon bow for the finishing touch.

Eastern Paradise

- Peach Gladiolus
- Red Lilies
- Orange Nerine
- Peach Carnations
- Red Oak Leaves
- Leatherleaf fern

Attach a frog to the bowl using floral fix then firmly wedge the floral foam in place. Create the triangular line of the arrangement using leatherleaf fern, placing the tallest piece at the back and bringing the sides down. Put more stems round the base, covering as much foam as possible.

Working in groups, add two sprigs of *Gladiolus* to the left of the centre and one at a horizontal angle to the right. Next add three orange nerines to the right of the centre, using the tallest at the rear, and three red lilies of differing heights at the centre front. Add more leatherleaf to cover the foam if necessary.

Trim the rose stems to the required length, varying each one to prevent regimentation. Slit up the cut stems and crush them gently before pushing into the foam. Use the longest rose at the bottom corner and work in a loose line up the centre left. Cover any remaining visible foam with rose leaves.

Add the peach carnations to the right to balance the roses. Vary the length as before, adding a few individual tall stems to the centre right. Curl strips of florist ribbon by running them against the back of a pair of scissors. Attach the end to a stub wire wrapped with florist tape and insert between the roses and lilies.

Radiant Reds

- Red Gerbera
- White Spray Carnations
- Red Tulips
- Red Carnations
- Christmas Tree Fir
- Holly
- Fruit and nuts

Fix a soaked floral foam firmly in a plastic dish using a frog stuck to the dish with floral fix. Push the end of a candle into the centre of the foam and then add Christmas tree fir, stripped of lower leaves to prevent them rotting in and crowding the foam. Place the fir horizontally, working all round the base.

TIP
- Never leave lighted candles in an unattended room and always arrange so that the candle wick is well above the top of flowers.

Add carnations to the base of the foam, above the fir. Use longer stems at either side to emphasise the line and bring shorter stems to the front and rear, working round so that it looks equally good from all angles. Add holly, preferably with berries, to cover the foam top, again following the elongated line.

Add three red gerbera in a line through the centre, and then five tulips, three horizontally and one either side of the candle. Next place carnations in a slightly diagonal line from side to side. Add oiled ivy leaves, bunched fruit and nut decorations round the centre. Place two white carnations in the centre as a foil to the red flowers.

Make three tartan ribbon bows using a yard (metre) of ribbon cut into equal lengths. Starting 8in (20cm) from one end, make a loop, pinching together between thumb and finger. Continue making five more loops, pinching all the centres together, and then secure by twisting one end of a stub wire round the centre. Finally wrap the stub wire in floral tape to prevent water damage.

Push stub wire into the centre of a cone, hold securely with thumb and twist round some cone petals to secure the wire in place, then anchor in the floral foam. Add the larger cones to the base and smaller cones to the centre. The ribbon bows, tucked into available space, and imitation parcels attached by stub wire add to the festive feel of the arrangement.

Stand this arrangement either on a pedestal or on a table, allowing the foliage to flow naturally.

Spaghetti Blues

- Gypsophila
- White Stocks
- Monto Casino
- Dyed Dill
- Blue Delphiniums
- Blue Iris
- White Spray Carnations
- Carnations (dyed blue)
- Eucalyptus Leaves
- Leatherleaf Fern

Use webbed ribbon to make decorative loops held in place with taped stub wire.

Colour the water to match the choice of blooms by adding blue ink or food colouring. Then firmly seal the spaghetti jar with a candle cup wedged into the rim with a seal of floral fix. Attach a frog to the centre cup and impale a block of soaked floral foam on it.

Working diagonally, and in groups, make the outline shape. Use eucalyptus leaves angled down to the left, and the monto casino diagonally opposite, allowing them to fall naturally. Fill in between with *Gypsophila*. Next add dyed dill in a lower diagonal line to the right. Cover any visible foam with leatherleaf fern.

Place the blue delphiniums over the eucalyptus leaves to the left, letting them fall naturally to create a shower effect. Work round to the rear as well, so that the display can be placed in the centre of a table and viewed from all angles.

TIP
● Carnations soak up dye fairly easily, so an alternative to spraying them is to stand them in water mixed with any food colouring. If using coloured water for the arrangement, carnations will gradually change colour anyway.

Add spray carnations in a loose diagonal line through the arrangement. Next spray three white carnations with florist dye to match the blues. Place centrally, together with three white stocks, to make the focal point. Mix five blue iris in with the monto casino, filling out the shape.

Simple Silhouettes

- 5 Longii Lilies
- Ruscus Leaves

When arranging even a few flowers in a vase, it is advisable to use chicken-wire or floral foam to keep them in position. Cut the chicken-wire to the correct height so that it sits just inside the lip of the vase, then coil it to fit snugly. Fill the vase with water to within 1¼in (3cm) of the top.

TIP
- Use an odd number of flowers, for instance three, five, or seven, as this will help to create the right balance.

Add flower food, which will extend the life of the flowers, before positioning any blooms. Trim the lower leaves from the *Ruscus* to prevent them rotting in the water and then place three stems in the vase, so that one is at either side and one is to the rear, forming a triangle.

Strip the lower leaves from the five longii lilies, placing the tallest at the rear, three centrally and one at the front, stepping the heights down in stages. Push into place gently but firmly to prevent the stems from splitting. Adjust the lily leaves once the stems are in position and add further *Ruscus* leaves if needed to fill out the shape.

PROJECT 18

Pretty in Pink

- Gypsophila
- Pink Carnations
- Pink Nerines
- Pink Spray Carnations
- Leatherleaf
- Eucalyptus Leaves

Cut soaked floral foam to size and pack tightly into the container, leaving a small gap at the rear for daily watering and at least 3in (8cm) of foam standing proud. Using leatherleaf and eucalyptus leaves, begin to shape the outline, working evenly round the arrangement. Cover as much of the floral foam surface as possible.

Cut three pink nerines to different heights, placing the tallest in the centre, flanked either side by two smaller blooms. Using sprigs of *Gypsophila*, work round the display filling in the shape. Use the *Gypsophila* cut into separate pieces to place more easily.

Working round the base, make a lower edge using five stems of spray carnations cut into individual blooms, then add pink carnations round the centre. Position two taller carnations either side of the nerines to fill out the shape. Finally, use spray carnations to fill any remaining gaps.

TIP
● Add trims to suit the occasion. Here, bootlace ribbon has been looped six times and held in place with taped stub wire for an unusual effect.

St Clementine

- Yellow Roses
- Cream Carnations
- Cream Freesia
- Peach Gladiolus
- Peach Nerines
- Orange Lilies
- Ruscus
- Cyclamen Leaves

To open rose buds or other soft blooms, either blow gently into the centre of the bud just before adding it to the arrangement, or gently fold out the outer petals using thumb and index finger.

This display is forward facing so that it can be placed against a wall. Wedge a soaked floral foam into the container, leaving 1½in (4cm) standing proud so that flowers can be placed horizontally as well as vertically. Using the *Ruscus* and cyclamen leaves, start the triangular outline placing the tallest at the rear.

Starting at the left side, use cream carnations to define the shape. Cut to varying lengths, insert the tallest in the centre left, followed by a line down the front. Working in the same way, insert more carnations diagonally down the side, finishing horizontally. Add five roses and finish with yellow freesias grouped at the front.

To balance the left side, add the peach flowers to the right, using the two tallest *Gladiolus* in the centre, and following the line down the centre front with peach nerines. Finish the line with the shortest nerine placed horizontally. Fill the right side with orange lilies, again working down in a diagonal line.

PROJECT 20

Petite Posy

- Roses
- Delphinium
- Silver Leaf
- Sprig of Money Tree

TIP
- Use any left-over flowers and pips in a co-ordinated little dish, adding another dimension to the display.

Cut the soaked floral foam and wedge it into a dish. Using a knife, slice away the top half of one side of the foam to form a ledge. Place the sprig of money tree at a slight angle in the centre of the top foam. Use smaller leaf stems to follow round the dish shape and place one small stem in the centre of the lower ledge.

Add the top of the delphinium to the lower ledge, cutting the stem slightly longer than the opposite money tree sprig. Surround the base with delphinium 'pips' covering the foam surface. (A pip is a single flower head snipped from the stem and used separately.)

Use three small roses in the base of the left side, filling in the remaining gaps with silver leaf. To secure small pieces, use short stub wire lengths bent into pins. Add a bootlace coil made from narrow ribbon to bring out the pink in the delphinium.

White Lights

- White Spray Chrysanthemums
- Bracken Ferns
- Leatherleaf

Cut the soaked floral foam to fit the white container, leaving about 3in (8cm) standing proud. Attach foam to a frog firmly stuck into the dish base. Next cover the foam surface with leatherleaf. Use four bracken fern leaves to define the triangular outline, placing two back-to-back vertically in the centre and one horizontally either side.

Add five spray chrysanthemums, cutting the ends at an angle and splitting up the stems to increase the drinking surface. Only cut off the very lower buds and leaves to prevent rotting and then place the chrysanthemums horizontally around the base.

Add the remainder of the chrysanthemums to the display, working up towards the middle with one tall spray at the centre. To fill any spaces, trim some bud stems from fuller blooms and place in the gaps.

Cut 2in (5cm) wide florist ribbon into ½in (1cm) strips, and then curl by running the back of a pair of scissors firmly down the length of ribbon. Wrap stub wire with floral tape starting at one end, twisting the wire and gently stretching the tape as you go.

Twist one end of the taped stub wire round the ribbon curl to hold it in place. Then add the ribbon curls to the arrangement, placing them amongst the flowers in any remaining gaps.

TIP
• To make the arrangement circular, simply use 20 spray chrysanthemums and mirror the steps above for the other side.

Woodland Urn

- Pyracantha Leaves
- Bracken Fern
- Ruscus
- Eucalyptus
- Silver Leaf
- Rose Leaf
- Cupressus
- Ivy

Fill the urn to the top with water and then wedge half a floral foam brick in the neck so that the underside is immersed. Leave a gap at the back for daily watering. Start with the eucalyptus leaves, place upright in the centre and work down to the right. Use *Ruscus* and ivy leaves angled to the lower right, allowing them to drape naturally. Place one stem upright at the centre.

Cut the lower end of a stem of *Pyracantha* and place the longest part angled down to the left, with the shorter part slightly above to add depth. Place a second stem upright to the left of the centre, pushing stems through the foam into the water. Add bracken ferns and then cupressus to fill in the left triangular side.

Add a single bracken fern to the lower right to balance the shape. Use about five top pieces of rose leaf, spray with leaf shine and then place in the front at a slight diagonal line from left to right. Finally, add a cluster of silver leaf to the centre front as the focal point.

Any foliage can be used to create this type of display; simply choose leaves that match your décor. *Ruscus* and leatherleaf fern are good basics with which to start. Pushing heavy stems through the foam into the water will give them greater support.

Christmas Coppers

- Pyracantha
- Gladiolus
- Silk Poinsettia
- Carnations
- Roses
- Alstroemeria
- Christmas Fern
- Vine
- Holly
- Candles, Beads and Baubles

Cut a block of floral foam into two and wedge both pieces into a polished copper pan, slicing off the corners to neaten. Avoid water spilling over the sides when topped up. Use two types of candle, Christmas beads, baubles, metallic ribbon and Christmas fern.

Place the five thin candles, cut to different heights, in the left floral foam. Then place the three shorter candles in the right foam, again varying the height. Add Christmas fern round the base, covering the pan rim. Use two pieces of twisted vine to the rear, then cut the end tips of *Pyracantha* and insert at the front with a stem angled as the handle.

Add holly to the right for balance. Place two *Gladiolus* next to the vines, using a longer stem at the back. Two silk poinsettias at the front balance the line, whilst a third tucked between the candles will cover the base. Then add three red carnations opposite the *Pyracantha* to complete the diagonal line.

Place three roses at a slight diagonal angle to the left front. Then use one stem of *Alstroemeria* split into six smaller lengths. Place three pieces either side to form an imaginary diagonal line across the display.

TIP
• To give leaves an extra shine either spray with leaf shine or rub with a little olive oil.

Twist silver rose wire between Christmas beads to stiffen and hold in shape and cut to desired lengths. Add baubles to the vine and metallic ribbon bows, as well as ribbon twirls and loops, held in place with stub wire wrapped in floral tape to prevent water damage.

Breath of Spring

Half fill the vase with water, adding flower food to prolong the life of the flowers. Starting with *Ruscus* and tree fern, outline the shape, letting the ferns fall naturally. Use the tallest *Ruscus* at the back and balance either side with euphorbia. This forms the basis of the arrangement and will help to hold flowers in place.

Cut the stems of the five iris at an angle to help water soak up to the blooms and then arrange them among the greenery to support the stems and keep them in place. Next add the five tulips, stripping away lower leaves, and placing each carefully among the iris.

- Tulips
- Iris
- Daffodils
- Narcissi
- Euphorbia
- Ruscus
- Tree Fern

Strip off the outer leaves before adding a few daffodils to the arrangement, filling in the spaces. Finally add narcissi, again placing in the gaps between other flowers. Push the stems right down to ensure they are under the water. Step away from the arrangement between adding each narcissus to see clearly where best to place them.

Natural Gold

- Gerbera
- Euphorbia
- Holly
- Ivy Leaves
- Bleached Fungi
- Dried Leaves and Flowers (seed heads)
- Bleached Vine

This stand is made very simply from a small block of wood, glued to two cube feet and then stained. Add floral foam, cut to size, to each small florist dish, wedging into place and then securing with florist tape across the centre and round the base. Stick each dish to the stand using floral fix.

Using ivy leaves cover the sides of the left floral foam, with a large dried leaf across the base. Add a tall twisted vine to the rear and a second vine to the side. Surround with gerbera, placing the tallest at the back, stepping down to the shortest at the front. Use a large ivy leaf at the rear to complement the vines.

Separate candle wicks and push them into the right floral foam. Attach bleached fungi using stub wire or dressmaking pins to hold in place. Add three dried seed heads to the front, placing two upright and one horizontally. Next use two small stems of euphorbia horizontally at the front and to the right.

Add ribbon to one side and baubles to the base of the candles for the final festive touch. The shot silk ribbon used here has fine wire through the edges so that it can be gathered as desired, twisting the surplus wire to hold it in position. Alternatively, gather the edges using a loose gathering stitch. Fix to the foam with covered stub wire.

TIP

● To make the stub wire pins that are used to hold fungi in place, simply cut stub wire into 4in (10cm) lengths and bend double into the shape of hairpins. Push the pins through the fungi and into the floral foam to anchor in position. Use as many pins as necessary to secure the fungi.

● When using pins on fungi, avoid pinning the edges which can flake away easily.

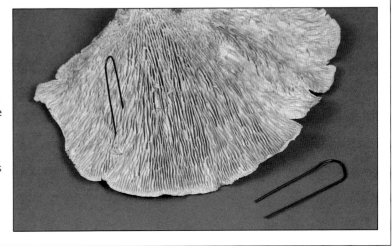

Tied Continental Bouquet

- Garden flowers
- Roses
- Gerbera
- Odd leaves from the garden

TIP
● To support weaker stems, cover the stub wire with green floral tape, push it into the back of the flower head and twist gently down round the stem.

This tied bouquet is arranged in the hand and then tied, ready to put straight into a vase. Start with one long stem of foliage and a long-stemmed rose. Twist floral twine round both these stems two or three times to start the tie which holds the bunch in place. Add another rose and two gerbera, twisting twine round once after adding each flower.

Continue adding flowers as desired, twisting the twine round after each flower is added. Also add more leaves to fill out the arrangement, letting them bend naturally, wrapping the twine round them as you go.

Holding the bouquet firmly between fingers and thumb, add odd leaves to the left-hand side and front, securing once again with a twist of twine each time. Finally, add a ribbon bow to the right-hand side to balance the shape.

PROJECT 27

Rose Posy

- Roses
- Cyclamen Leaves
- Tree Fern
- Posy frill

Attach the frill to the base of the posy holder, using pins pushed into the dry floral foam. Cut cyclamen leaves at a 45-degree angle to make them easier to insert into the foam and then add them in a ring, equally spaced round the base.

Trim three rose stems to about 3in (8cm), stripping away leaves. Add to the centre of the posy, placing them in a loosely vertical line. Place sprigs of tree fern between the cyclamen leaves to fill out the surrounding base.

Add the remaining roses, placing each carefully to form a rounded, shaped posy. Use more cyclamen leaves, cut to a mere 1in (2.5cm) in length, to cover the foam surface. Extra tree fern can also be added to any spaces between the roses. Finally place the three bows around the centre roses, together with a long trail of matching ribbon.

To make ribbon bows (1 yd (1m) makes three bows), cut the ribbon into equal lengths. Starting about 10in (25cm) from one end, create a loop crossing over from left to right in a figure-of-eight. Repeat until five loops have been made. Pinch the centres together and bind with covered stub wire. Finally, trim the ribbon ends to the desired lengths.

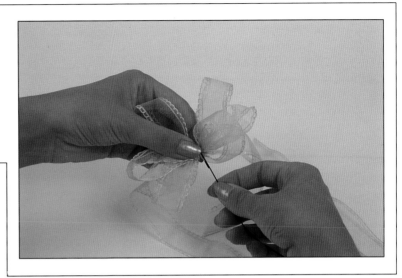

TIP
● Use green wire or tape the stub wire with waterproof floral tape.

Gift Bouquet

- Peach Spray Chrysanthemums
- Orange Spray Carnations
- Yellow Carnations
- Yellow Chrysanthemum Blooms
- Cream Spider Chrysanthemum
- Gypsophila
- Leatherleaf

Make the bouquet wrapping from a 6½ft (2m) piece of clear Cellophane cut from a roll (available from florists). Fold in half lengthways, then fold the left side edges over about 1¼in (3cm) and staple together to form one side of the bouquet bag. Leave the other side open whilst arranging the flowers.

Open the unsealed edge of the Cellophane and place the leatherleaf in the centre. Next add spray chrysanthemums working in groups of three, starting with the tallest at the centre. Continue to add layers, placing a large chrysanthemum in the centre, then three yellow carnations and three orange spray carnations. Finish this stage with a sprig of *Gypsophila*.

Next layer the remaining two chrysanthemum blooms with the rest of the spray chrysanthemums. Add more *Gypophila* before the final orange spray carnations. Bring the top layer of Cellophane back over and then fold the edges and staple together. Scrunch the bottom edge together and tie firmly with the remaining strip of ribbon. Add the tied bow to finish.

Following the instructions on page 5, make a florist bow using 10ft (3m) of polypropylene ribbon. The secret of making a successful bow is to hold the band tightly in one hand, pulling and twisting each loop out firmly.

Dutch Advent Wreath

- Holly
- Pine Leaves
- Ivy
- Cupressus
- Red Carnations
- Bonn Moss
- Gold Silk Poinsettia
- Fir Cones
- Baubles, berries, candles

Thoroughly soak a foam-based wreath ring before beginning. Spray paint the candles with gold paint and wire the artificial berries together in groups. Also add covered stub wire to the baubles so that they are ready to anchor in the foam. Make ribbon bows, securing with taped stub wire.

Trim the pine leaves into individual fronds and, working with them upside-down to show the silver side, place them round the outer edge to create a frill. Make a similar frill round the inner edge using single fronds of cupressus. Add four painted candles at the 'quarter hour'.

Trim away the underside of the Bonn moss and pin four pieces at intervals to the foam ring using pins made from stub wire. Working round the display, add sprigs of holly. Attach stub wire to cones to secure in place and *one* to each candle base together with the artificial berries.

Add the gold silk poinsettia or other colourful ornament at intervals. Place three red carnations facing towards the centre and trail one or two ivy lengths through the display. Finally, add baubles and bows, placing single baubles around the outer edge and a bow at the base of each candle.

To anchor cones in place, twist a stub wire around the cone about 12in (30cm) from the base. Twist the two ends together to secure and then wrap the remaining ends with taped stub wire.

TIPS
- Follow the Dutch tradition and light one candle each Sunday in December, finishing with all four on the last Sunday.
- Spray the moss daily to keep it moist.
- Use some fresh flowers if preferred, replacing them when necessary.

Tied Bouquet

Prepare all stems in advance, trimming at an angle for better water absorption and stripping away lower leaves. Lay the prepared flowers and foliage on a table so that they are easily reached, as one hand will be needed to hold the bouquet as it progresses. Start with some leatherleaf and a sprig of *Gypsophila*.

Next add the flowers, starting with a rose in the centre. Add two more roses, turning the bouquet round as you add each stem, thus working in a spiral motion. Then add a spray of carnations, all the time holding the bouquet firmly in one hand.

- Roses
- Gypsophila
- Spray Carnations
- Spray Chrysanthemums
- Leatherleaf

Add spray chrysanthemums, still working round, holding the stems together firmly. Add more leatherleaf and *Gypsophila* as you are turning the bouquet, pulling the *Gypsophila* heads among the other flower heads. Add an outer layer of spray carnations and roses, before a final backing of leatherleaf. Trim all stems to an even length and then bind securely with florist ribbon.

Prepare the circular Cellophane doily by folding it in four to make a triangular shape. Cut a section out of the corner, unfold and push stems through the hole. Gather the Cellophane round the stems, tape to hold and then add a looped florist ribbon bow. When in place, tear the long ends into strips and curl them by running along the scissor edges.

TIP
● When preparing a tied bouquet as a gift, also wrap the stems in Cellophane to preserve the moisture longer.

Bridal Bouquet

- Spray Carnations
- Roses
- Alstroemeria
- Gypsophila
- Ivy Leaves
- Trailing Ivy

Gather together the flowers and foliage that you wish to use for this flowing bridal bouquet, preparing the stems in the usual way. The posy holder can be held either way up, so it is important to decide how it is to be held before starting the design.

Twist a light silver wire round single ivy leaves to secure round the base of the posy holder. Add pieces of trailing ivy to define the shape, length and height; again using silver wire round the end to secure it to the dry foam ball. Spray the leaves with leaf shine.

Add the first spray carnations to the lower end of the bouquet, cutting each stem to a different length, and place the longest first, working up to the shortest. Next add three roses following the same line as the carnations, pointing the first blooms downwards and bringing the line up through the centre. Add a diagonal line of spray carnations.

Add more roses, stripped of lower leaves, following the original line through to the top. Add two more, one either side of the central rose. Trim individual stems of *Alstroemeria* to about 2½ in (6cm), strengthening the ends with silver wire to hold securely in place. Add these to the outer centre of the foam ball. Tiny sprigs of *Gypsophila* added to the base fill out the shape.

Make ribbon bows by cutting 20in (50cm) lengths, looping and twisting in the centre. Secure with stub wire wrapped in floral tape to prevent water damage. Add the bows as desired. Finally add a long twirl of ribbon, again securing with covered stub wire, to the bottom of the bouquet so that it follows the line of the design.

Cradle Designs

- Matacaria
- Singapore Orchids
- Spray Carnations
- Pink Rose buds
- Leatherleaf

Soak floral foam thoroughly before wedging firmly into the cradle. If necessary, line the cradle with a polythene bag before adding the foam. Select ribbon to match the container and flowers that are in proportion, such as tiny-headed matacaria, spray carnations and pink rose buds.

Insert leatherleaf into the floral foam, following the shape of the cradle, and use the top tips of leatherleaf, placed horizontally, to cover the foam base. Cut three stems of Singapore orchids to varying lengths, place round the cradle following the outline already started. Use the top of the stems to define the finished length.

Trim the pink rose buds to different lengths between 3–6in (8–16cm), splitting the stems about ½in (1.5cm) to help water absorption. Place in a line from back to front, going under the handle with the taller blooms at the back. Use rose leaves either side to fill out the foliage and provide contrasting colour, thus emphasising the flowers.

Keeping to the shape already defined, cut the matacaria to about 2–4in (5–10cm) lengths and use to fill between and round the roses and orchids, providing the bedding of the cradle. Next add the spray carnations round the roses, filling any remaining gaps.

Cut the ribbon into 20in (50cm) lengths for the matching bows. Make four loops holding the centre firmly between thumb and fingers, leaving two long edges. Hold together with a twist of covered stub wire. Add to the arrangement as the finishing touch.

Baby Blues

TIP

For a girl use pink chrysanthemums and freesias instead of the blue flowers.

- Brodiaea
- Gypsophila
- White Roses
- Spray Carnations
- Dyed Deep Blue Chrysanthemums
- Ruscus
- White Feathers

Fix a frog securely to the stork base with floral fix and then push a soaked floral foam into position. Trim *Ruscus* to varying lengths, placing round the base front to define the bird's breast. Place soft white feathers among the *Ruscus* round the base to follow the stork theme. Add a couple of extra feathers to the tail end.

Cut the *Brodiaea* to about 3in (8cm) and place among the feathers, working all round to maintain the shape. Add extra *Brodiaea* cut into longer lengths of about 4in (10cm) to the tail end in order to emphasise the tail effect.

Trim roses to between 4–6in (10–15cm) and place in a line from head to tail, starting with stems placed horizontally, working up and over, leaving the longest rose for the tail end. A single rose at the front will balance the line. Add sprigs of *Gypsophila* to fill in the shape, working round and over the whole base. Cut the spray carnations to single blooms and add to the centre.

To finish, add the sparkling dyed blue chrysanthemums round the arrangement. Trim to single blooms about 3in (8cm) high in order to keep their height slightly below that of the roses. Fill any remaining gaps in the body section with one or two more feathers. Using about a yard (1 metre) of ribbon, add bows to the centre and another multi-looped bow to one stork leg.

TIPS

- To colour chrysanthemums coat them with floral spray paint (available from florists).
- To add glitter, spray flower heads lightly with spray glue and then sprinkle with glitter.

PROJECT 34

Bathroom Bubbles

- Tulips
- Single Daisy Chrysanthemums
- Gypsophila
- Leatherleaf

Wedge the soaked floral foam into the neck of the jug, leaving a gap for watering, and then fill with water to within 1¼ in (3cm) of the rim thus ensuring the foam base stays immersed in water. Use the leatherleaf to cover the floral foam and begin the outline shape. Add six tulips, cut to about 10in (25cm), round the sides, allowing each bloom to fall naturally. Place another tulip upright to the rear to define the height.

Add sprays of *Gypsophila* for a frothy soft effect. Work across the centre of the arrangement and round the lower front of the base. Continue to add *Gypsophila* until the display is nicely rounded and looks soft and flowing.

Trim spray chrysanthemums to varying heights to get the best from each spray, but keep them shorter than the tulips which have already defined the height of the arrangement. Use the buds and flowers placed among the *Gypsophila* to fill out the centre. Use single blooms from long stems to fill any gaps.

Add three more tulips, opening out the petals by lightly running the outer petals between thumb and fingers, one at a time, gently bending each one outwards. Place in the centre of the display.

Fireside Glow

TIP
● Copper or metallic leaves are available from florists but, unfortunately, usually only at Christmas.

● **Single Red Chrysanthemums**
● **Carnations**
● **Spray Carnations**
● **Lilies**
● **Sprayed copper leaves**

ace a plastic pot inside the brass container to avoid narking and spoiling the brass. Add soaked floral foam, sing a whole block in the centre with two shorter blocks the sides. Add the sprayed copper leaves to define the oft triangular outline, placing the first stem upright at the ear, working down through the front and round the base.

Cut the single red chrysanthemums to varying lengths, keeping each spray whole, and add to the display following the outline already made. Place the tallest stem upright to the rear, working down both sides and front, using the shorter stems at the centre front.

eep the carnations fairly long, but strip off the lower aves. Then brush open the heads by blowing gently into hem and place them round the outer edge and through ne centre. Use spray carnations to fill out the roundness nd soften the triangular line, by placing them next to the arnations and among the red chrysanthemums.

Finally, add the six stems of lilies, stripping the lower leaves and pinching out stamens which can stain if they drop on to furniture. Use the lilies to fill out the centre front and provide an eye-catching focal point.

First published in 1994 by
The Crowood Press Ltd
Ramsbury, Marlborough
Wiltshire SN8 2HR

British Library Cataloguing-in-Publication Data

A catalogue record for this book is available from the
British Library.

ISBN 1 85223 639 6

Picture credits

All photographs by Lez Gardiner and Graham Cooper.

Typeset by Acorn Bookwork, Salisbury
Printed and bound by Paramount Printing Group, Hong Kong